2
93

DISCARD

94

DATE DUE

PRINTED IN U.S.A.

Where Animals Live

The World of Rabbits

Text by Jennifer Coldrey

Photographs by
Oxford Scientific Films

Gareth Stevens Publishing
Milwaukee

Where Rabbits Live

Rabbits can live almost anywhere, if it is not too hot or too cold.

Rabbits often live in and around the edges of fields.

Here is an alert rabbit at the edge of a field.

Rabbits like to feed in grassy meadows. They especially like *pastureland*. There, the grass is kept short by grazing sheep or cattle.

They like *cultivated* fields, too. Rabbits sometimes do damage by eating crops that farmers grow.

Rabbits are shy and hard to find in the day.

But they leave many signs that they are around — like the fur caught in this bush and this tunnel in the grass! ➡

Warrens

Many rabbits live together in family groups. Their underground home is a network of tunnels called a warren.

The warren has several entrances and exits. Some are very small *bolt-holes*. The bolt-holes are only 2½ inches wide. This makes them too small for many *predators* to use.

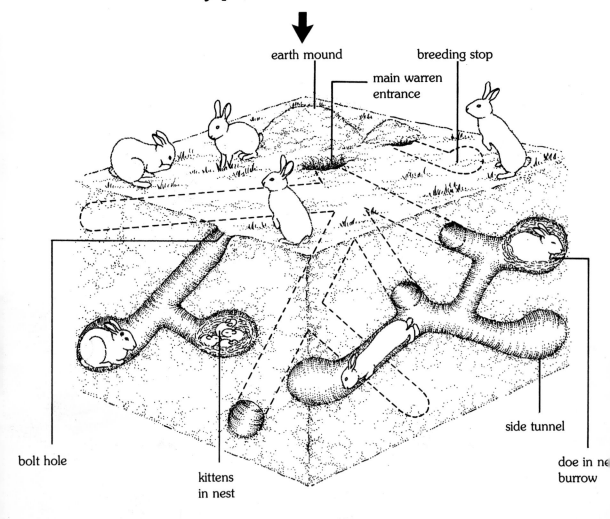

earth mound

breeding stop

main warren entrance

bolt hole

kittens in nest

side tunnel

doe in ne burrow

Warrens are easy to find. The entrances are marked by mounds of dirt. Here a young rabbit peeps out from a bolt-hole.

Warrens are safe, warm places. Here rabbits sleep, digest their food, and take care of their babies. As rabbits breed, the number of tunnels in a warren grows.

The Rabbit's Body

Rabbits come in many colors. European rabbits (below) have greyish-brown fur on top and white fur underneath.

Rabbits *molt* their fur once a year, starting in the spring. By fall, they have a new thick winter coat.

A male rabbit (called a *buck*) looks much like a female (called a *doe*). Bucks may be a little bigger than does. Here, the doe is on the right.

North American Cottontails look a lot like European rabbits. But they make their homes in the grass or under bushes and rocks, instead of underground.

Rabbits have big eyes and long ears. They have very good eyesight and hearing.

Rabbits constantly sniff and twitch their noses to pick up smells in the air.

Rabbits have two kinds of teeth. The front teeth are called *incisors*. They are for cutting and biting. The back teeth are called *molars*. They have flat, ridged surfaces and are for grinding and chewing. The teeth never stop growing. But they are kept short as the rabbit chews on trees.

Legs and Movement ↑

Rabbits do not run or walk. They jump or hop along the ground.

◄ Their front legs are small and good for digging. Their back legs are longer and stronger for jumping.

Rabbits can hop very fast. At high speeds the back legs land ahead of the front ones. Their tracks often show this! ↓

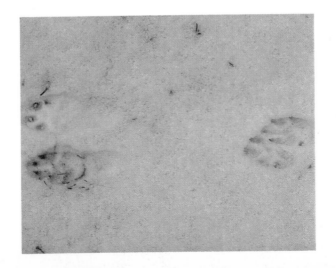

Food and Feeding

Rabbits eat plants and feed mostly at night. But they sometimes come out in the daytime to feed in quiet fields.

Plant-eating animals eat lots of food! A rabbit can eat at least one pound of green food per day. But rabbits are also choosy eaters. They like short grass and tender young shoots.

Rabbits are out all year. In winter, food is hard to find. So rabbits often eat the bark off of young *saplings*. This causes serious damage to the saplings.

Digestion

Rabbits eat mainly at night. After they eat their fill, they return home to digest their meal.

Plants are hard to digest. They also do not provide enough nourishment when they pass through the rabbit's *intestine* just once.

That is why the rabbit eats its first droppings, which are soft and moist. This way, the food passes through the intestine twice.

The second droppings are dry. They are left above the ground when the rabbit comes out at night.

Behavior

Rabbits are very clean animals. They spend lots of time washing themselves. And they never litter their homes with droppings.

Rabbits wash their fur by licking it. They also brush it with their paws.

Rabbits hardly ever wander very far from their homes. Even at night, they stay close to the safety of their burrows.

During the day, rabbits rest. If it is warm, they may stretch out and enjoy the sunshine.

Social Life

Most rabbits live in large groups or colonies. Sometimes several hundred rabbits may live together inside a large warren!

In each family group, the oldest buck protects the does and young ones. A buck marks his *territory* with a scent from a *gland* under his chin. He spreads the scent by rubbing his chin on the plants in his territory.

Bucks do so much of this "*chinning*" that they often rub all the fur off of their chins.

During the breeding season the bucks become aggressive. Sometimes they even fight for the does or the territory. The fights can end in death for the weaker buck.

Does rarely fight. But they can be aggressive when they are protecting their young.

Mating and Breeding

A buck usually mates with more than one doe. He courts the female by dancing in small circles. If she is interested, she joins in the dance.

When she is ready to mate, the doe lets the buck climb on her back, and they mate.

After mating, the doe makes a nest for her babies. She uses grass, moss, leaves, and even fur from her own belly!

The baby rabbits are born four weeks after mating. They have no fur, and they cannot see or hear.

Growing Up

Rabbits grow quickly. They reach adult size by the time they are nine months old. And does can breed by the time they are only three or four months old! Even baby rabbits grow fast. By the end of the first week their weight is doubled, and they have fur.

By twelve days, the rabbit kittens' eyes are open.

This rabbit is three weeks old. Now it is ready to explore the world around its home.

These young rabbits are four weeks old. They are fully *weaned*. Now their mother will leave them to take care of themselves.

↑

Predators and Other Dangers

Rabbits are killed and eaten by many animals.
Their natural enemies include foxes (above),
weasels (below), badgers, stoats, rats, dogs, and
both wild and domestic cats.

↓

Large birds of prey like buzzards (above), hawks, eagles, and owls swoop down on rabbits from the air.

All of these predators are especially dangerous to young rabbits. They are not as strong as adults. Also, they are not as quick. Many are also killed by cold, disease, or starvation. Most baby rabbits die before they are one year old.

Defense

Rabbits are weak and timid. They cannot easily
defend themselves, so they must be alert to signs
of danger.

They can also signal DANGER to each other. One
way is to thump their back legs. They may also let
out a high-pitched scream when they are scared
or hurt.

When danger is near, rabbits lie low in the grass
with their ears laid back.

Rabbits usually stay close to some sort of cover.
This way, they can escape when danger
threatens. Also, their fur helps give them
camouflage and makes them hard to see.

Rabbits and Humans

People have had a great effect on the lives of rabbits. Humans have helped rabbits spread all over the world. People also hunt rabbits, both for sport and to keep their numbers down.

In some areas, ferrets are used to chase rabbits out of their burrows.

Sometimes diseases spread through whole populations of rabbits. Unfortunately, humans have also used these diseases to control the overpopulation of rabbits.

In the 1950s, a *virus* carried by fleas (below) was used in Europe. It killed practically all the rabbits in Britain. Luckily, some rabbits escaped and were able to keep on breeding.

Friends and Neighbors in the Fields

Many other animals share the *habitat* of rabbits. One neighbor is the hare. Hares are close cousins of rabbits. But all hares live alone and stay above ground. Hares are bigger than rabbits, and they cause less damage because they eat less. Also, hares do not breed as fast as rabbits.

↑

Some animals, like this hedgehog, may make their homes in empty rabbit burrows. And rabbits in turn may use empty burrows of other animals.

Rabbits also share pastureland with grazing cattle and sheep. Rabbits like to eat grass that has been kept short by these animals. ↓

Life in the Fields

Rabbits depend on plants to build up their bodies and to give them energy. In their turn, rabbits are an important food supply for predators. In this way, rabbits are an important link in a food chain.

The Food Chain

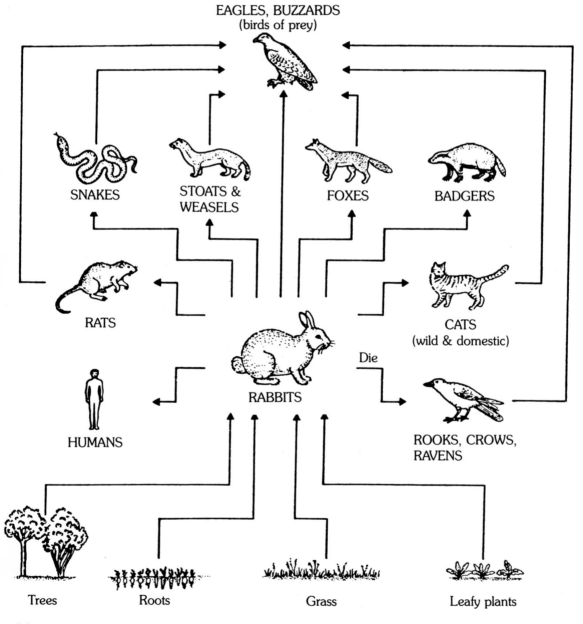

EAGLES, BUZZARDS
(birds of prey)

SNAKES

STOATS &
WEASELS

FOXES

BADGERS

RATS

CATS
(wild & domestic)

HUMANS

Die

RABBITS

ROOKS, CROWS,
RAVENS

Trees

Roots

Grass

Leafy plants

Rabbits eat the crops of farmers, and their digging spoils good land. In turn, modern farming methods and *insecticides* can hurt rabbits and their habitats.

Few wild rabbits live past two years. And yet, rabbits do survive. They are alert, and they breed so quickly. After all, one pair can produce millions of descendants in only three years! Is it any wonder they have survived?

New Words About Rabbits

These new words about rabbits appear in the text in italics, just as they appear here.

bolt-holes . . . . small holes through which to escape
buck . . . . male rabbit
camouflage . . . . . . animal disguise; how an animal hides by looking like its surroundings
chinning . . . . rubbing the chin against plants or the ground to leave a scent
cultivated . . . . used for growing crops
doe . . . . female rabbit
gland . . . . part of the body that makes special liquids such as sweat, milk, or digestive juices
habitat . . . . the natural home of any animal or plant
incisors . . . . long, sharp, cutting teeth at the front of the rabbit's mouth
insecticides . . . . . . poisonous chemicals which people spray on crops to protect them from insects
intestine . . . . part of the digestive system below the stomach
molars . . . . back teeth of rabbits (and all other mammals) which are used for crushing and grinding food
molt . . . . to shed hair or fur and replace it with a new coat
pasture(land) . . . . grassland used for grazing sheep or cattle
predators . . . . animals that kill and eat other animals
saplings . . . . young trees
territory . . . . piece of land which an animal defends against intruders
virus . . . . microscopic organism which causes disease inside animals or plants
weaned . . . . (of young animals); no longer dependent on their mother's milk for food, but now able to eat other things

Reading level analysis: SPACHE 2.2, FRY 2. FLESCH 88 (easy), RAYGOR 3, FOG 4, SMOG 3

Library of Congress Cataloging-in-Publication Data

Coldrey, Jennifer.
  The world of rabbits.

  (Where animals live)
  Summary: Simple text and photographs depict rabbits feeding, breeding, and defending themselves in their natural habitats.
  1. Rabbits — Juvenile literature. [1. Rabbits] I. Oxford Scientific Films. II. Title. III. Series.
QL737.L32C65 1986   599.32'2   85-28988
ISBN 1-55532-089-9
ISBN 1-55532-064-3 (lib. bdg.)

North American edition first published in 1986 by
Gareth Stevens, Inc.
7221 West Green Tree Road   Milwaukee, Wisconsin 53223, USA

First conceived, designed, and produced by Belitha Press Ltd., London, as *The Rabbit in the Fields,* with an original text copyright by Oxford Scientific Films. Format copyright by Belitha Press Ltd.

The publishers wish to thank the following for permission to reproduce copyright material: **Oxford Scientific Films Ltd.** for pages 2 *below right,* 6, 7 *below left,* 8 *above* and *below,* 9 *above* and *below,* 10 *below,* 11 *above* and *below,* 12, 13 *above* and *below,* 14, 15, 16 *below,* 17, 18 *above* and *below,* 19 *above* and *below,* 20 *above* and *below,* 21 *above* and *below,* 22 *above,* 24, 25 *above* and *below,* 26 *above* and *below,* 29 *above,* and 31 *left* and *right* (photographer G. I. Bernard), page 1 (photographer P.K. Sharpe), page 2 *above* (photographer Raymond Blythe), page 2 *below left* (photographer David Cayless), page 7 *above* (photographer M. P.L. Fogden), page 10 *above* and 27 (photographer David Thompson), page 16 *above* (photographer Chrissie Houghton), page 22 *below* (photographer Avril Ramage), page 29 *below* (photographer Sally Foy); British Natural History Pictures for pages 3, and 7 *below right* (photographer John Robinson); Aquila Photographics for page 23 (photographer Dennis Green); Survival Anglia for page 28 (photographer Dieter Plage). Front cover photographer: G.I. Bernard. Back cover photographer: David Cayless.

Typeset by Ries Graphics ltd.   Printed in Hong Kong
U.S. Editors: MaryLee Knowlton and Mark J. Sachner
Design: Treld Bicknell   Line Drawings: Lorna Turpin
Scientific Consultants: Gwynne Vevers and David Saintsing